MORE THAN THESE

MORE THAN THESE

A Book of Poems to Encourage and Inspire

DESMOND E. R. OTTLEY

AuthorHouse™
1663 Liberty Drive
Bloomington, IN 47403
www.authorhouse.com
Phone: 1-800-839-8640

© 2011 by Desmond E. R. Ottley. All rights reserved.

No part of this book may be reproduced, stored in a retrieval system, or transmitted by any means without the written permission of the author.

First published by AuthorHouse   10/03/2011

ISBN: 978-1-4670-4388-5 (sc)
ISBN: 978-1-4670-4387-8 (hc)
ISBN: 978-1-4670-4386-1 (ebk)

Library of Congress Control Number: 2011917713

Printed in the United States of America

Any people depicted in stock imagery provided by Thinkstock are models, and such images are being used for illustrative purposes only.
Certain stock imagery © Thinkstock.

This book is printed on acid-free paper.

Because of the dynamic nature of the Internet, any web addresses or links contained in this book may have changed since publication and may no longer be valid. The views expressed in this work are solely those of the author and do not necessarily reflect the views of the publisher, and the publisher hereby disclaims any responsibility for them.

THE SOURCE

The underlying Source that enables my poetry writing is contained in these words: "It is not that I think that I can do anything of lasting value by myself. My only power and success come from God."

(2 Corinthians 3:5—New Living Translation)

DO

    YOU

        LOVE

            ME

MORE

    THAN

        THESE?

(John 21:15)

Dedicated to

DOLLY, MY DARLING WIFE of 54 years,
without whose loving care, support, patience,
and encouragement this book would not have
been possible;

and

MY FOUR GRANDCHILDREN,
Simone, Melyssa, Gavin Jnr and Desmond Jnr,
who have been a blessing to me;

and

MY THREE GREAT-GRAND CHILDREN,
Jahziyah, Jaelen and Channiah,
whose spoken and unspoken questions and responses never cease
to amaze me.

May God continue to bless you all.

Contents

The Source v

Dedication vii

Foreword xi

Acknowledgements xiii

Section 1—Lessons From Nature 1

Section 2—Lessons From The Strangest Birth 11

Section 3—Lessons From The Greatest Life 21

Section 4—Lessons From The Costliest Passion 41

Section 5—Lessons From The Miraculous Rising 51

Section 6—Lessons For Daily Living 63

Index Of Meters, Titles And Scriptural References 116

Foreword

I felt as if the only relief I could get would be to stop breathing. But how does one stop breathing just to keep living?

It was my second day home from hospital where I had my appendix removed about a week earlier. I began feeling a discomfort in my chest around midday, and as the day wore on the discomfort grew into a severe pain. It did not help that I was alone, my spouse having gone to work. Having a dear someone near at hand always seems to diminish pain and discomfort in some inexplicable way. When my pain grew to an unbearable level, Dolly and I decided I had to return to the hospital. With her at my side, I was admitted. I could see from the facial expressions and comments of the nurses and doctors around me that the situation was critical. The continuing pain in my chest also confirmed that.

Later in the evening when I found myself alone in my hospital room for the rest of the night, a feeling of foreboding came over me. It was the very first time in my life that I genuinely thought that I may not be alive to see the next day. That thought scared me no end, and I began to think of my family and my unfinished life. What will happen to my son and my spouse? What will happen to . . . ? What will happen when . . . . ? What will happen if . . . ? Then, as I was taught to do by my parents during my younger days, I did it. What do you do when you don't know what to do? You pray and ask for divine guidance.

After I prayed, I suddenly saw things in a completely different light. It seemed so very clear to me that it did not matter what happened to me. Whether I lived to see the next dawn or not, everything was going to be alright with me and with my family. I relaxed, thanked God, went to sleep and slept like a baby.

Ever since that night, that experience has helped me to be a more obedient follower of Christ, and to trust more deeply in God's love and promises, regardless of what life throws at me. Since that night I've used as one of my faith-guiding one-liners John Newton's words: "'Tis mine to obey, 'tis His to provide".

It is my genuine hope that, with the help of the Divine Creator, these poems will help to lift each reader's life to a new level of faith, commitment and trust in God where, despite the circumstances, you will be able to use the words of William Cowper (1) as your own testimony.

> "Though vine nor fig-tree neither
>   Their wonted fruit should bear,
> Though all the field should wither,
>   Nor flocks nor herds be there,
> Yet, God the same abiding,
>   His praise shall tune my voice;
> For, while in Him confiding,
>   I cannot but rejoice."

For those of my readers who love to sing, it may interest you to know that each of the poems may be sung to a hymn tune. In the index at the back I have listed the meter of each poem. You simply have to find a hymn tune with the same meter and sing to your heart's content.

Singing or not, enjoy and be inspired.

Note 1: Hymn #527: From the *Methodist Hymn-Book With Tunes*. 34th Edition, 1962

Acknowledgements

I would like to acknowledge the other sources which have provided ideas and inspiration for many of the topics developed in these poems.

My initial attempt at writing poetry was prompted by my admiration for the beautiful music I heard from the North Toronto Collegiate Institute's senior choir and orchestra directed by the late David Beaton and David Ford respectively. This was at the 1972 annual Maytime Melodies performance. My next strong desire to write a poem grew from the urging of my friend Cicely Grell-Hull to use a well-known tune at a performance by the St. Kitts-Nevis Choral Group during its tour of St. Kitts & Nevis. Encouraged by the choir's enjoyment in singing this poem, I wrote a few more and began to search and listen for ideas that could be developed into poems. Thank you Mother Cicely and my faithful choir members.

I am grateful to my darling wife, Dolly, whose patience and encouragement allowed me to spend many thinking hours in an undisturbed atmosphere both day and night whenever I chose.

I am also grateful to my niece Carol Mitchell whose occasional words of encouragement pushed me to apply greater effort towards the completion of this book.

Several persons in their sermons and prayers at the churches I've attended, by their use of a particular word, or phrase, or sentence, spawned in my own mind parallel but different ideas that I was able to develop into a poem. To these persons who unknowingly on these occasions aroused my own thinking, I express my gratitude.

Finally I want to thank Chris Toring and Elliott Devolin at Authorhouse, for their patient guidance and suggestions as I tried to steer a proper course between completing the poems and getting the book published.

My deepest thanks to all of you for your kind support and much appreciated encouragement and assistance. Blessings on each of you.

SECTION I

LESSONS FROM NATURE

(1) THE BEAUTY OF GOD'S WORLD

The beauty and order in nature are met
In vivid examples all round us; and yet
We take them for granted, their value ignore,
And oft disregard them as sand on a shore.

The crocus, the tulip, the bright daffodil,
The snowdrop, the iris, the peony, the squill,
All these in their season start flowering on cue,
Most wondrously signaled when their time is due.

The white apple blossoms, the promise of fruit,
The young thorn-filled rosebush fresh sprung from
    the root,
The busy nest-building by birds on the wing,
Proclaim with assurance the arrival of spring.

The hummingbird hovering the nectar to take,
Rough stones water-smoothed at the edge of the lake,
The rose-colored sunset, the starlit night sky,
Are signatures of the Designer on high.

The order and beauty we see in our world
Exist not by chance. They are God's flag unfurled
To signal to all who are willing to see
The scope of Omnipotent Divinity.

(2) ROADBLOCKS

Go to the ant. It has a skill profound
    To persevere.
It goes straight through, above, below, around;
    It shows no fear.
It never will give up or seek retreat,
When it encounters roadblocks at its feet.

The tender root, obstructed in its growth,
    Detects a crack.
Pushing and growing, gently it does both
    To keep on track.
Unyieldingly advancing without sound,
When it encounters roadblocks in the ground.

The salmon swims upstream to reach the place
    Where it was spawned.
Southward birds fly, oft at a strenuous pace,
    Just to be warmed.
They never will give up even for a day,
When they encounter roadblocks in their way.

Whenever you begin life's hill to climb
    To reach a goal,
Foes will arise to challenge life and limb
    And vex your soul.
Resist the urge to quit. Just persevere.
Trust in the One who bids you "Have no fear".

(3) WATER

It cleanses each blemish, it quenches the fire,
It purges the impure, yet fashions deep mire.
It nourishes life that would otherwise die,
Yet, left uncontrolled, creates reasons to cry.

When clean, it refreshes and promotes new growth.
When stagnant, it harbours the pests which we loathe.
Controlled, it produces much good for our use;
Unbridled, it spreads such disastrous abuse.

Like water, we all are the carriers inside
Of virtuous goodness which cleanses life's tide.
But goodness won't issue unless we ensure
It's garnered in vessels kept wholesome and pure.

Such wholeness and purity can only be
Supplied and sustained when, with honesty, we
Submit our whole self and relinquish our claim
To personal goodness, and trust just His Name.

Like water, we surely can nourish the ground
Where wholeness is lacking and discord is found.
But we can spread poison around us if we
Live life with abandon and set our tongues free.

As water flows gently through valleys and rifts,
Disposing of refuse, depositing gifts
Of health-giving moisture, so we can improve
And moisten the world in our corner with love.

Desmond E. R. Ottley

If sadly our life becomes sullied, be sure
It can be renewed and made clean as before.
As vaporized water is turned into rain,
Our lives can be changed and made useful again.

(4) CONSIDER THE STARS

Stupendous height, amazing depth
Beyond our comprehensive view;
Such unimagined length and breadth
So far removed from what we knew.
The worlds beyond our tiny sphere
Affirm the Maker's marvellous care.

From any point on our fair earth,
Thousands of stars we can behold.
They form one vast galactic berth
With billions more, so we are told.
Can we e'er grasp the Maker's power,
The same that cares for us each hour?

Our universe, the scholars say,
Consists of these vast mysteries.
For every grain of sand that lay
On earth, there are ten galaxies.
Who can perceive such boundless space?
'Tis boundless as the Maker's grace.

The One whose power such space designed,
Is the same One whose life was spent
To rescue me. Let now my mind
Trust the Divine Omnipotent.
Who dares to spurn the One whose face
Keeps watch o'er such unending space?

Matchless Creator, holy Lord,
Unrivalled Architect divine,
Open my eyes, empower your word,
That I may know all power is Thine.
May I acknowledge that your love
Is endless as the space above.

(5) SALT

O God, Creator without fault,
Who gives each living being its worth,
You have declared we are as salt
That richly flavours life on earth.

Through your kind grace and matchless power,
We can, like salt, enrich the taste
Of daily life each passing hour,
For those whose lives are touched by waste.

Give us the wisdom to preserve
The willingness to live for You.
That we may always seek to serve,
And spread our love like morning dew.

Help us to live, to strive, to pray
That always we'll be close to you.
So that whate'er we do or say,
Will mirror what you'll have us do.

Give us the strength to do what's right.
Give us deep longing to assist
All those who falter in the fight
To thrash sin's foes whom they resist.

At times when our own fervour fades,
When strenuous efforts bear no fruit,
Help us to lift the hindering shades
To let God's love play like a flute.

Desmond E. R. Ottley

May we persist in offering aid
To all whose need we can relieve.
May we, despite the outcomes feared,
Spread spiritual salt through life's great sieve.

SECTION 2

LESSONS FROM THE STRANGEST BIRTH

(6) THE CHILD FROM BETHLEHEM

'Twas on a bed of manger hay
He lay when He was born;
Not in a palace splendidly
Bedecked with gold that morn.

'Twas to some shepherds in the fields,
Not rulers of the day,
That angels told the joyful news
And sang their tuneful lay.

His parents were of lowly breed,
His home no king's delight.
Yet threats against His life were fierce,
And led to secret flight.

His birth was part of God's wise plan
To right humanity's wrong.
Yet we reject the effectual cure
Promised through ages long.

We strive and toil with restless zeal
Life's ills to overcome;
We wrestle with, and worry o'er
The storms that touch our home.

We oft forget the reason why
The Babe of Bethlehem
Was sent to earth that winter's night,
A fragile, heavenly Gem

Desmond E. R. Ottley

It was to give light to all those
Who in death's shade do sit,
And guide the feet of them who seek
To have life's torch relit.

O may we now rededicate
Our lives, each treasured gem,
To Him who patterned love for hate,
That Child from Bethlehem.

(7) IT CHANGES EVERYTHING.

Amazed, she listened to the words
That deeply touched her soul.
"You'll bear a Son" whose life would fill
A predetermined role.
"How can that be?" she gently asked
The radiant angel guest.
His answer touched her faith-filled heart.
She knew God's will was best.

From that day forth her life was changed.
She pondered in her heart
The trust that God had placed in her,
How best she'd do her part.
It mattered not what others thought,
How difficult or rough
The road ahead would be for her.
God's trusting was enough.

God's will so oft disturbs our life
With sudden urgency,
Giving new purpose to our thoughts,
As 'twas for young Mary.
The child within changed everything;
New compass and new chart.
Trusting in God's most sacred word,
She lived with a pure heart.

That's how it is when Christ comes in
And takes His rightful place
Within our lives. We abhor sin
And fully trust His grace.
Whene'er we think of Jesu's birth
And joyful carols sing,
Let's not forget He came to earth
To be our Lord and King.

Let us in all things seek His will,
And His just rule obey.
In word and deed, desire and thought,
Let us walk in His Way.
As helpless as a child He came
To show us how to live.
We now must honour His great name,
And our best worship give.

(8) NO ROOM

Our Wonderful Saviour, Redeemer and Counsellor,
Was born in a manger where animals fed.
His parents exhausted and weary with travel
Could find no safe place to lay his infant head.

"No room!" That's the message so silently given,
When we have no moments to spend with our Lord.
When hours are consumed with demands for our attention,
We're left at day's end with an impaired record.

What is it that robs us of time for devotion?
Is it our weak faith that God's promise is true?
'Tis written: "Seek first the true kingdom of heaven,
And all needed things will be added to you."

Go forth now with new faith. You've been with the Christ-child.
Like magi, return by a new way to life.
Avoid evil influence and spread wholesome incense,
The myrrh of compassion, the gold that spurns strife.

(9) THE KEY TO YOUR HEART

Weary and famished from such a long journey,
Needing no more than refreshment and rest,
All she could get was a spot in a manger
Hardly befitting such kingly a guest.

Princes and monarchs are hosted in splendour,
But all He got was the baa-ing of sheep.
Though hailed by angels as Prince above princes,
Mother and child on rough straw had to sleep.

Still, after centuries of hearing about Him,
How He cured people and sighted the blind,
How He was crucified and was arisen,
He is rejected with treatment unkind.

Let not desire to flourish displace Him.
Let not your pride cause your faith to depart.
No better thing can you do but receive Him.
Give Him first place and the key to your heart.

(10) EVEN IN A DREAM

Sometimes we're forced to make a serious choice,
When circumstances clash with deafening voice.
We may take action but remain unsure,
Still searching for assurance and much more,
    Even in a dream.

Like Joseph we may ponder and decide;
Delay would worsen the oncoming tide.
But like him we should willingly apply
The counsel when it comes from God on high,
    Even in a dream.

Sometimes we are so focused on a plan
Which we've researched at length as best we can,
That we are blind to dangers lurking round,
And miss the warning signs that can be found
    Even in a dream.

Like the Wise Men we boldly seek our goal,
Not conscious of deceptions we've been sold.
But like them we should willingly apply
The counsel when it comes from God on high,
    Even in a dream.

How oft grave danger lies outside our door,
Threatening our homes although we feel secure.
We live oblivious to the signs that show
Great peril's near. We miss the warning glow
    Even in a dream.

In all things may we confidently trust
That in our crisis times the True and Just
Will surely resupply our every need,
And furnishing heaven's aid, will intercede,
    Even in a dream.

SECTION 3

LESSONS FROM THE GREATEST LIFE

(11) QUESTIONS OF JESUS

Even though the crowd was pressing
    Round You near the billowy sea,
You still sensed the need that reached You
    When you queried: "Who touched Me?"
When we find life's woes oppressive
    And we struggle for relief,
Make us mindful of Your question;
    Keep us free from unbelief.

As You taught the truths of heaven,
    Doubters found it hard to stay.
But You challenged Your disciples:
    "Will you also go away?"
When our faith becomes diluted
    By rejection of God's word,
Make us mindful of Your question;
    Keep us loyal to You, Lord

When ten men received Your healing,
    Only one did take the time
To return to thank and praise You.
    Hence You asked: "Where are the nine?"
When our days are filled with blessings,
    And our life's cup runneth o'er,
Make us mindful of Your question.
    Keep us thankful evermore.

Desmond E. R. Ottley

As You dined on that bright morning,
    With disciples now at ease,
Lovingly You asked of Peter,
    "Do you love Me more than these?"
When the gems of earth delude us,
    And our love for You grows cold,
Make us mindful of Your question.
    Keep us safe within the fold.

(12) CLAIMS OF JESUS

I am the Door. I bid you boldly enter,
    Trusting in Me, even when all efforts fail.
No longer will defeat ensure surrender,
    The Door gives hope that surely you'll prevail.

I am the Way, the Truth, the Life. O Listen!
    You need not stay upon the path you tread.
If satisfaction and real joy evade you,
    Follow My Way and live true life instead.

I am the Bread of Life. The food I offer
    Will strengthen and equip you for the strife
Which you must face each day and each tomorrow.
    Seek now My nourishment for deeper life.

I am the Vine. You are My precious branches.
    Vainly you try to bear fruit all alone,
For without Me you can indeed do nothing.
    Abide in Me. Ask and it will be done.

(13) INVITATIONS OF JESUS

Come unto Me, you that are spent and weary.
    You need not sink 'neath loads you find too heavy.
Put on My yolk! It's easier to carry.
        Come unto Me, now.

O Come and Dine, if for My food you hunger.
    I will supply your needs, your faith make stronger.
Life's crumbs need not suffice you any longer.
        O Come and Dine, now.

Take up the Cross and follow Me in earnest,
    Willing to sacrifice all you hold dearest.
You who would fight for truth, to Me are nearest.
        Take up the Cross, now.

Come ye apart with Me. Leave stress behind you.
    Busyness jades. Spurn the duress around you.
Spend time with Me each day, strengthen within you.
        Come ye apart, now.

(14) WHAT MANNER OF MAN

He is so peacefully asleep
Astern, inside the boat.
But stormy winds threaten to sweep
Away His friends, who strive to keep
Their sinking craft afloat.

He wakes, and with serene control
He calms the boisterous main.
The angry waves now cease to roll.
His wakeful presence calms each soul;
All is at peace again.

How oft, mid scenes of quietness,
Fierce storms abruptly rise
To threaten all our dreams, and press
Upon our lives extreme distress,
Demanding actions wise.

When thus oppressed, we trust that One—
Our tempest-calming Friend.
Whether we've lost a dear someone,
Or cruel circumstance hits home,
We trust right to the end.

If even the wind and waves obey
God's voice, why should we fear
What life will throw at us each day?
Why hesitate our vows to pay?
We're in God's constant care.

Desmond E. R. Ottley

(15) TO WHOM SHALL WE TURN?

Our plans and goals, even though well managed,
Don't always work out as they should.
Disruptive forces leave them damaged
Depleting what was meant for good.

We toil preparing for the future
With goals well crafted and devised;
We plan ahead; high hopes we nurture,
Yet oft our plans go unrealized.

The flow of life, so unprotected,
Silent as light, dogged as time,
Slides circumstances unexpected
Upsetting plans, even dreams sublime.

A great career replete with promise
Is wrecked due to one careless deed.
A happy home with wholesome practice
Is marred by one infectious seed.

A friend, a spouse, a son or daughter
Is taken home beyond the sky.
An empty space begging their laughter,
Is left behind in hearts that cry.

When times like these are filled with sadness,
What can we do? Where do we turn
In our attempt to regain gladness?
Is there a lesson we can learn?

More Than These

We can do what our sane thoughts tell us,
Attempt the best that we can try.
But lingering hopes in steady chorus
Still each day drain our spirits dry.

We can, not seeking explanations,
Turn to the ONE who holds the key
To life's mysterious, puzzling questions,
The One who said: "Come Unto Me."

We pray that God will give direction,
Supply the needs, open the door
That shows the path to full correction,
And give us wisdom to endure.

(16) BY THE WAYSIDE

Two blind men by the wayside
Sat waiting hopelessly,
Bombarded by the noises
Of all that passed them by.
Ignored and disregarded,
Day after day they sat
In fruitless boredom, waiting
To gain, they knew not what.

'Tis easy to sit waiting;
'Tis easy to postpone
Taking that needed action
That gets the sought goal won.
'Tis easy to be blinded,
Though eyes are open wide,
By attitudes and habits
That leave deep wounds inside.

Are you among those waiting
Along life's wayside drear,
Oblivious to the chances
Available each year?
If only you'll gain freedom
From crippling sloth's control,
You'll find new strength and purpose,
New compass for your soul.

More Than These

Why waste a life of promise?
You've many a river to cross.
High mountains wait your climbing;
Don't let all chance be lost.
You've races begging contest;
You've battles to be fought.
Bestir yourself! Take action!
Don't spend your life for naught.

Great gifts to you were given
At birth. Don't let them lie
Like weak unwatered seedlings
That wither, shrink and die.
Begin to live with purpose;
Waste not another day.
Set goals; plan their fulfillment,
And on this new path stay.

Don't rue your life's inaction.
Move boldly towards your goal.
Be honest, just and kindly.
Seek nurture for your soul.
Trust your Divine Creator;
In His great love abide.
Leave your soft-cushioned station
Down by the old wayside.

Desmond E. R. Ottley

(17) HIS GARMENT'S HEM

For twelve long years she sought a cure,
Resulting in an empty purse.
Physicians' remedies no more
Were helping her, for she grew worse.
Her hope was spent, despair rose high,
Until that day the Lord passed by.

With mounting hope she pushed her way
Through jostling crowds to where He stood.
She knew by faith that on that day
She would be healed and healed for good.
If she could touch His garment's hem,
To her that would be diadem.

She touched, and instantly was healed.
Her pain, her shame, her waiting, gone.
Divine empowerment did yield;
Her simple act of faith had won.
Who can explain the quick transfer
Of virtue, straight from Him to her?

Our lives are sometimes hemorrhaged sore
By ruptured veins of selfish thought.
Such simple wounds, fetid, impure,
Expose our lives to ills unsought.
But could we touch His garment's hem
Our faith would bring us diadem.

More Than These

No longer need we pine and fret
When sickened by misfortune's woe;
If we but trust, we still can get
The healing strength to thrive and grow.
Let's touch in prayer His garment's hem.
For us that will be diadem.

(18) THE PITCHER OF WATER

Can Jesus trust your faithfulness
To do what He desires?
Or can He trust your willingness
To go where He requires?

He sent two of His trusted friends
To look for someone bearing
A water pitcher. "Follow him".
He'll lead you to the building.

If he who bore the pitcher then
Had failed to take the water,
The trusted friends may not have found
The room for that Last Supper.

He did the very mundane chore
That Jesus had expected.
And thus he helped fulfil the plan
That Jesus had selected.

Have you been faithful day by day
Performing deeds of kindness,
That seem too simple and too small,
Too trivial and worthless?

Have you been tempted to postpone
Giving the help intended
To one who seemed to be in need,
The one whom you befriended?

More Than These

It may be that the simple gift
That you were moved to offer,
Was just the help she needed most
If she was not to suffer.

Don't underestimate the worth
Of simple acts of kindness.
Your action may be just the wedge
That lifts the scales of blindness.

So if you're urged to offer help
That trivial seems, and simple,
Don't hesitate to follow through.
Give that sad face a dimple.

It may be that you are the one
Some needy soul is seeking
To lead them to their Upper Room,
Where they'll receive Christ's blessing.

You must live faithfully to be
Acknowledged as Christ's follower.
Let your light shine; with gladness bear
Even just your pitcher of water.

Desmond E. R. Ottley

(19) AS I

Jesus is our great example
As we walk the Christian way.
From His life we can learn lessons
That will boost our faith each day.
He said "Keep my clear commandments
As I've kept" my Father's laws.
If we do, we'll live much better
As disciples of His cause.

Such obedience will require
Constant aim and daily prayer.
Such will be an antiseptic
To the evil lures we fear.
We will also need to firmly
Re-arrange our settled life,
So there's no day when we ever
Do forget Christ in our strife.

Jesus gave in clearest language
A commandment for our guide.
"You must love each other dearly,
As I've loved you. See my side."
Touch His tender hands, both piercéd;
Feel the blood-drops from his wounds.
Hear the anguished cry: "Forgive them!"
Was there e'er such love-filled sounds?

More Than These

We are called to be obedient
To God's word in holy writ.
We are called to love each other
Just as Jesus modeled it.
If the Christ with all His power,
Loved us and obeyed God's word,
We must follow His example,
If He is to be our Lord.

(20) THE AMAZING CHRIST

Sick and weakened, frail and dying,
Barely able even to talk,
He sought healing from the Master,
But was told to stand and walk.
Though unable, he was able.
Christ empowers those who obey.
May I trust the healing Saviour
To enable me when I pray.

At the wedding feast in Cana,
The supply of wine went dry.
"Fill the waterpots with water
To the brim" was Christ's reply.
Though 'twas water, wine was tasted.
Christ can watery lives re-wine.
I will trust the powerful Saviour;
To Him I'll my life resign.

In the temple on the Sabbath,
One man had a withered hand.
"Stretch it forth" the Master told him.
He obeyed this strange command.
Though unable, he was able.
Christ empowers those who obey.
Even in my weakest moments,
I'll trust Christ to show the way.

More Than These

If life's stresses are disabling,
Stunting hopes and pruning dreams,
Should attempts to make life fruitful
Falter, smashing plans and schemes,
Turn to Christ who waits to give you
The unspoken strength you need.
You will find Him true and faithful
If each day you let Him lead.

SECTION 4

LESSONS FROM THE COSTLIEST PASSION

(21) WHAT A FRIEND

Have no fear when life's arrows strike you,
Have no fear when your best plans fail,
Have no fear when your hopes do not prevail.
Keep in mind that Christ conquered failure,
Keep in mind that He rose again,
Keep in mind that He triumphed over pain.

Do not fear if your friends betray you,
Do not fear if you feel alone.
Do not fear if the good you've done
Is cast away like stone.
Think of how some His friends betrayed Him,
Think of all the pain He bore,
Think of how He said "I am the Door".

Trust in Him when strong doubts besiege you,
Trust in Him when praise turns to jeers,
Trust in Him when no answer comes to prayers.
He's the One who cried out "My Father,
Why hast Thou forsaken me?"
He's the One who faced scorn upon the tree.

Now He lives having won the victory
Over life, evil and the grave.
Now He lives in the seat of power
Ready to heal and save.
Jesus lives. We now have a champion
Sworn to help us to the end.
Praise, thanksgiving, honour! What a Friend!

Desmond E. R. Ottley

(22) WATCH WITH ME

In times of sorrow and distress,
When mauled by pain or loneliness,
We ache for comfort and release.
Nothing on earth helps like the kind
Uplifting solace that we find
When caring from close friends increase.

At times like these we sometimes turn
From friendship's balm, and wrongly spurn
The very ones whom we need most.
We struggle in our grief and pain,
Forgetful of the peace we gain
When friendship's lessons are not lost.

When saddened at Gethsemane
Our mighty Lord said "Watch with Me,
I need you near for one brief hour."
He could have summoned heavenly force,
But earthly friends was His own choice
To compliment the Father's power.

When days are dark and life is tough,
When doors shut tight and roads get rough,
When all seems lost and storm clouds lower,
Let close friends rally to your side,
But keep in mind that Jesus died
Depending only on God's power.

(23) THE DAY BETWEEN

O the depth of pain and anguish
Heaped upon one guiltless soul.
Cruelly tortured, left to languish,
One who made so many whole.
O what grief! Quenched belief!
On each side a dying thief.

O the joy of resurrection!
Someone rolled the stone away.
Under planned divine direction,
Good did triumph that first day
Of the week. Staunchly meek,
He now reigns o'er strong and weak.

But betwixt defeat and victory,
Was that day that fell between.
Death on one side, life the other,
Witness to the human scene.
So will we surely be
Touched by life's infirmity.

When life's sharpest arrows strike us,
Leaving us deprived of hope,
When it seems that we're defeated,
At the end of our short rope,
Let's recall, though we fall,
Days between are life's firewall.

Desmond E. R. Ottley

Don't despair though pain or failure
Clouds your path in what you do.
Just ere dawn the night is darkest;
Comes relief when it is due.
You will see, wondrously,
Love Divine your Help will be.

(24) THE OTHER JOSEPH

He was not the one whose father
Gave a coat with varying hue.
He was not the one whom angels
In his dream said: "This you'll do.
Take the young child and his mother,
Flee to Egypt and stay there."
But this Joseph was a counsellor,
Born in famed Arimathæa

He, no doubt, was surely present
When false witnesses accused
The Just One who was on trial,
Him who cruelly they abused.
Yet this Joseph kept his silence,
While the lies flew without end.
But when death at last took over,
He took action for his friend.

It is sad that in our culture
Still in Joseph's shoes we walk.
We heap tribute upon tribute
To the dead with saddened talk.
We ignore their lifeless station;
We pretend that they can hear.
How much better had we spoken
While they lived among us here.

Desmond E. R. Ottley

Though this custom is unsettling,
It gives comfort, without doubt,
To all those who mourn the passing
Of the one whose light winked out.
By the tributes, we remind them
How that life, in many ways
Fostered good in countless others,
Justifying belated praise.

Let's not save our flowers and tributes
Till our loved ones take their leave.
Let's not withhold commendations
From all those who should receive.
Let us genuinely give plaudit
To all those who touch our lives.
While they live, let us deposit
Praises, ere death shuts their eyes.

More Than These

(25) I WAS THERE

When Jesus died, who were the guilty culprits
That helped to hatch such vile conspiracy;
The ones who by the fruits of their lulled spirits,
Brought to a boil such awful agony.

Scripture has pointed the accusing finger
At certain naméd persons who were there.
But though I surely was not there to linger,
Could I have contributed my fair share?

Have I not shown indifference, as did Pilate,
Who could have ruled "Acquitted! He is free."
But fearing censure, he condemned the Inmate.
Have I been braver for my Lord than he?

Have I been devious like the sly Caiaphas,
Who, though he held the office of High Priest,
Incited other holy men to trespass?
Have I been faithful to those who count least?

Have I not been unfeeling as the soldiers
Who jeered and mocked as painfully He hung?
Have I e'er blocked with words and hurtful boulders
The path of some whose lives have just begun?

Have I e'er fostered a revengeful spirit
That, mob-like, helps to drown compassion's voice?
Have I been slow to challenge and revisit
The thinking that in me creates poor choice?

Have I been fearful, as were the disciples,
Of what would happen if I spoke the truth?
Have I dismissed the bad effect of ripples
That would result if I lied to some youth.

Yes! I was there. But though I watched in silence,
Not knowing that my life was in plain view,
He spoke these words with such divine insistence,
"Father forgive! They know not what they do".

Such wondrous love! Unfeigned, unmatched forgiveness,
Dispensed on me, the one for whom He came.
How can I spurn this undeservéd goodness?
From henceforth I shall glorify His name.

SECTION 5

LESSONS FROM THE MIRACULOUS RISING

(26) ON THE ROAD

There was an urgent pacing in their walk,
A sense of hopeless feeling in their talk,
As they recalled the awful cruelty
That they had witnessed on the middle tree
     At Calvary.

Their Master's life among them for three years
Had raised their hopes and answered many prayers.
It seemed that finally relief had come.
But then their rulers' wicked hate struck home
     At Calvary.

So often in this life we build our dreams,
We plan our strategies and craft our schemes.
But then great disappointments intervene
And ruin all our hopes, as was the scene
     At Calvary.

In times like these do we, like them, immerse
Ourselves in grief, and mournfully rehearse
Our woes, with clouded minds and shuttered sight,
Forgetful of the Being who won the fight
     At Calvary?

Even when the Risen One with ardent breath
Explained the Word which had foretold His death,
So drenched in grief, they did not recognize
The One, the Crucified, who gained the prize
     At Calvary.

Desmond E. R. Ottley

How oft when danger looms, and storm clouds lower,
When faith itself seems so bereft of power,
The Risen One stands ready by our side.
But hope-dimmed eyes see not the One who died
    At Calvary.

Whether you suffer pain or deep distress,
Dashed hopes or tangled life, or helplessness,
Turn to the One who walks beside you now,
Who for your sake endured a thorn-pierced brow
    At Calvary.

(27) LIFE'S EARTHQUAKES

Earthquakes are often caused, some experts say,
    By sudden shifts
Deep in the earth, where cracks and fissures lay,
    And treacherous rifts.
Whether these shifts are gradual or intense,
They leave small room for mounting a defence.

Over the years as earthquakes took their toll
    On human life,
We've treated them as part of nature's role,
    An endless strife.
But when life's quakes disturb, destroy, derail
Our ordered lives, and rend our guarded veil,

We look for reasons why the incident
    Happened to us.
We search for ways to counter and prevent
    A repeat thrust.
But private earthquakes may be signs that God
Has intervened, imposed His potent rod.

Fettered and bound, they sang and prayed all night,
    And they were heard.
The earthquake opened doors and offered flight
    Without a word.
So in our human struggles, when we lean
On God, the Power Divine will intervene.

The very instant that our Dear Lord died
    The earthquake roared.
'Twas to proclaim that even when wrong tried,
    Good's victory soared.
At that sad hour, the earthquake signified
That death's vain transient grasp would be denied.

Whatever steals your joy or gives you pain
    Will be controlled.
When woes intensify and efforts wane,
    And hope grows cold,
Though earthquakes rock your life, trust in that One
Who, even over death, a victory won.

(28) STAY WITH US

As they walked closely with the gentle stranger,
They were so moved by all the things he told them,
That at their journey's end they wished he'd stay longer,
    And pleaded, Stay with us.

When we are troubled by events that bruise us,
When inner feelings cause us to need soothing,
When friends we've trusted, turn their backs and use us,
    Let us plead: Stay with us.

When spite our efforts to remain obedient,
We lose the closeness to the One we worship,
And to lukewarmness we become subservient,
    Let us plead: Stay with us.

When doubts perplex us and disturb out thinking,
When devilish arrows pierce our spiritual armour,
When our prayers languish and our faith starts sinking,
    Let us plead: Stay with us.

When we regret the angry words we've spoken,
When to forgive we fail, yet expect forgiveness,
When by our careless speech treasured bonds are broken,
    Let us plead: Stay with us.

When we see others whom we love and cherish
Trample core truths and live without discretion,
When causes we support start to wilt and perish,
    Let us plead: Stay with us.

Desmond E. R. Ottley

Boldly in faith let us make such petitions,
Assured the Risen One will not us abandon.
For He has promised, with few preconditions,
    Always to stay with us.

(29) AND PETER

As they went that early morning
On the first day of the week,
They were hopeless in their mourning,
But still came their Friend to seek.
What they saw filled them with fright.
Issuing from the one in white
Was a message plain and clear:
"He is risen! He's not here.

"Go tell the disciples quickly
They should wait in Galilee.
Be sure Peter knows that clearly
He too must wait there for Me."
Why should Peter get that word
After he denied the Lord?
O such wondrous love displayed
By the One who was betrayed.

In your life you may have suffered
Harsh betrayal, hurting sore.
Lies and insults 'gainst you uttered,
Dug deep wounds right to the core.
Others may have, with intent
Caused you pain, your spirit bent.
But 'tis foolish to compare
These, with wrongs Christ had to bear.

Desmond E. R. Ottley

God's free undeserved forgiveness
Reaches out both far and wide
To all those who mock His goodness,
Those by evil's cesspool dyed.
Slightest guilt or brutal wrong
Can be changed to healing song
By the matchless Power Divine,
Author of the rich Design.

Let us, using His example,
Our revengeful spirit tame.
Genuine pardon, free and ample,
We must practice in His name.
Matters not how deep the wound,
True forgiveness must abound.
Let us then with new intent,
Heed the news the angel sent.

(30) FOLLOW ME

At breakfast that day, after Jesus was risen,
They all were together with Him on the beach.
Although, after fishing all night, they caught nothing,
With loving forethought He provided for each.

At times when we've striven with fruitless exertion,
We get so depressed that our spirits grow weak.
But then Jesus comes and with wondrous precision
Provides what we need, just the strength that we seek.

He faced grieving Peter, and lovingly asked him
Deep questions intended to rouse his belief.
Then, probing more deeply, He challenged him further
And said "Follow Me", hoping to assuage his grief.

But Peter, who earlier confessed He was God's Son—
The Guardian of secrets, the Settler of strife,
Ignored this remarkably kind invitation,
His thinking distracted—a pitfall of life.

So, "What shall this man do?" This question is often
Conceived in our minds when our path we debate.
We needlessly ponder the fortunes of others,
Forestalling success in the plans we create.

When thus we lose focus, let us remain thankful
That we have a true Friend who walks by our side,
To challenge and nudge us back unto the pathway
Which leads us to where we can safely reside.

Desmond E. R. Ottley

Thanksgiving to You, everlasting Sustainer,
Who knows all our weakness, our faults and our need.
With Your grace allowing, and our hearts avowing,
We'll follow 'till death while on your love we feed.

SECTION 6

LESSONS FOR DAILY LIVING

(31) WE PRAISE YOUR NAME CREATOR

We praise your name Creator for every blessing given
To our small and humble nation, blessings sent down from heaven.
We thank You for peace and plenty, for freedom, sunshine and rain.
We give You thanks Creator for victory o'er strife and pain.

Lord, grant us courage to conquer every urge to do some wrong.
Forgive us each deed of passion that wrecks someone's song.
Give us the skill to listen; make us willing to pray.
May we be Christlike agents doing Your will each day.

Give to our leaders wisdom and grace. May all their motives be pure.
Give them keen insight, temper their deeds. Help them fair laws to secure.
We thank You blest Creator. We pledge our lives to You.
Strengthen us, mold us and fill us with purpose that's bold and new.

(32) YOU PROMISED LORD

You promised Lord, that You will always
    Hear our earnest prayer.
By Your example you have shown
    The level of Your care.
Enable us to live a life
    Of love, in word and deed;
And when we hear the cry for help,
    Supply each other's need.

You promised Lord, that You will always
    Guide when the way is dark.
When skies are black, you've sent the light,
    Forgiven when we've missed the mark.
Help us each day to shine like stars,
    And brighten someone's path.
Make us more willing to forgive,
    Returning love for wrath.

You promised Lord, that You will always
    Help the seekers find.
Open the door to those who knock,
    Give eyesight to the blind.
Give us the courage to support
    All those who knock and seek,
That they may find that open door
    Through which Your love will speak.

More Than These

We promise Lord, that we will always
    Give our very best.
Caring, forgiving, guiding the weak,
    Being kind to every guest.
Let every talent we possess
    And every strength we claim,
Work to relieve our neighbour's stress
    And witness to Your name.

Desmond E. R. Ottley

(33) AFTER THE WEDDING

May God's richest grace surround you,
    As you start this wedded life.
May your vows throw love-chords round you,
    Now that you are man and wife.

Hurtful deeds are now forgiven;
    Seek forgiveness when you're wrong.
Preference give one to the other;
    Be anger-free at set of sun.

When plans fail and expectations
    Dim, and joy gives way to pain,
Trust the Master of the nations
    Your composure to maintain.

Banish thoughts of getting even;
    Hurl resentments far away.
Speak the truth, confess mistakes, use
    Kind endearing words each day.

May you know divine contentment.
    Give God first place in your heart.
Pray you'll find that your commitment
    Will endure till death you part.

(34) PRAYER BEFORE BRUNCH

Loving God, our great Creator,
    Sure Provider of each need,
We confess there's no one greater,
    None forgives us each misdeed.
We acknowledge You as Maker.
    Prompt us all your laws to heed.

Thank You for Your wondrous guiding
    Of our Group these past few years.
Give us strength to keep providing
    Needed caring for our peers.
Give us wisdom in our living
    To dispel our needless fears.

As we meet on this occasion,
    To share laughter, food and fun,
Let us not remain unmindful
    Of the millions who have none.
Bless the meal and the preparers.
    This we ask through Your Dear Son.

(35) TRUST IN GOD

We often put our trust in things unseen.
    We trust the air is breathable and clean.
We trust that though the world is hurtling round
    At super speed, we will stay on the ground.
Why then do we not trust the written Word?
    "Fear not, for I have overcome the world."

Where darkness rules, light comes to show the way.
    Have you e'er seen two nights without a day?
In northern climes warm Spring gets rid of snow.
    We've never had two winters in a row.
Why then do we not trust the Word we read?
    "God will in time supply your every need."

When in a parent's care a young child lies,
    There is no fear of threats seen in its eyes.
When danger looms or foes come seeking food,
    The hen gives winged protection to its brood.
Why do we scorn the truth that we have learned?
    "Although you pass through fire, you'll not be burned."

When we build overpasses on our roads,
    We always fully trust they'll bear the loads.
We trust the pilot of the jumbo jet
    To bring us safe to journey's end. But yet
We spurn the One who gives this guarantee:
    "They will be safe who put their trust in Me."

More Than These

I kept the cruise of oil from running dry;
    The loaves and fishes I did multiply;
I rescued Daniel from the lion's den;
    I even gave My life for you. But then
Your doubts still hold you in captivity.
    I'm in control, My child. Just trust in Me.

(36) GOD'S LOVE, WISDOM AND POWER

Thanksgiving and praises
My grateful voice raises,
For God's love so lavishly poured out on me.
This love knows no ending;
It's constantly sending
All things that I need like a full flowing sea.

But love without wisdom,
Like a king without kingdom,
Though strong on intent, will both falter and wane.
God's love, though unbounded,
On wisdom is founded,
Ensuring no outcome but good from God's reign.

When love without limit
Has wisdom to guide it,
They bridled will be without power to act.
But here is the wonder;
Reject it no longer.
God's power can maintain love and wisdom intact.

Then boldly start giving
Your praise and thanksgiving
To God, the omnipotent, wise, loving friend.
He'll love you forever,
Abandon you—never.
The One who alone you can trust to the end.

(37) PRAYER FOR OUR NATION

Lord we gather here together
To give heartfelt thanks and praise,
For Your mercies, kind and tender,
Showered upon us through the years.
Make us humble lest we stumble.
Courage give to face our fears.

We confess that, as a nation,
Oft we've strayed from truth and right.
We deserve Your indignation,
Yet You've kept our future bright.
Make us thankful; keep us peaceful,
Always faithful in Your sight.

Keep our leaders wise and caring.
May they govern honestly.
Help us each in personal living
To uphold integrity.
May we harbour hate no longer;
From resentment set us free.

Grant our young ones wise discernment
To resist the lures they face.
May our families use wise judgement
At all times, in every place.
Keep us thriving in our striving,
Always strengthened by Your grace.

Desmond E. R. Ottley

(38) OVERCOMING

Life is full of joy and sorrow,
    Victory and defeat.
We can spurn or we can follow
    Either path we meet.
'Tis the Great Designer's choosing
    That our living be complete.

It is easy to be cheerful
    When the good winds blow.
But when days turn dark and tearful
    In disaster's throe,
Aspirations quickly crumble
    And hopes tumble very low.

From the lives of many a stalwart
    We can courage take.
We, like them, upon life's bulwark
    Our own stand can make.
Self-excusing, languid mettle,
    We can settle to forsake.

Blind George Matheson and Fanny Crosby
    Each penned many a hymn.
Blind Ray Charles and Stevie Wonder,
    Their songs we still sing.
Wilma Randolph, badly damaged,
    Gamely managed a gold sprint.

More Than These

Helen Keller, deaf and sightless
    Lived a life well planned.
Louis Vierne, that skillful organist
    Lacking sight and hand.
Itzhak Perlman, violin master,
    Polio disaster did withstand.

Terry Fox with cancerous lesion
    Won a nation's heart.
Vision impaired Karlene Nation,
    Makes her newscasts art.
Skilled Ruth Vallis, physiotherapist,
    A blind specialist in her craft.

All of these, without exception,
    Overcame great odds.
Painful truth and self-inspection
    Marked the road they trod.
We can follow their example,
    As an ample lightening rod

Desmond E. R. Ottley

(39) BREAKING DOWN BARRIERS

In this world of bold exploits
Many triumphs have been gained.
But some ventures pose a limit
Beyond which no crown is claimed.
Then upon the scene emerges
One who, with determined aim,
Breaks the barrier, and deposes
That which once defied acclaim.

Roger Bannister, noted athlete
Sprints the mile in under four.
Sylvia Earle, bravely untethered
Searches on the deep sea shore.
Lake Ontario yields its challenge
To the swimmer Marilyn Bell.
Edmund Hilary and Tenzing Norgay
Earn Mount Everest's victor's yell.

All of these by physical prowess
Have attained the victor's crown.
But fixed attitudes and habits
Pose strict barriers of their own.
They give rise to vexing problems,
Broken dreams and pain unsought,
Till we practice with insistence
What the Great Example taught.

More Than These

Banish "eye for eye" reaction;
In its place put "I forgive".
Shun resentment, spurn deception;
Boldly without malice live.
Treat all persons with compassion
As the Great Example showed.
In His strength, if you are willing,
Live life on the barrier-free road.

Desmond E. R. Ottley

(40) NAMELESS ANGELS

Sometimes a kind and noble deed
Brings good to someone's day.
The deed supplies an urgent need;
But, like the planted mustard seed,
The doer fades away.

The lonely widow, who, despite
Her lack of food, gave all
The oil within her cruse that night
To boost the prophet's strength and sight.
Her name none can recall.

The boy who gave his lunch to feed
Five thousand souls that day,
Gave all he had to fill their need
And, planting his small mustard seed,
Went nameless on his way.

The one who gave the widow's mite
Contributed her all.
Her act was like a sacred rite
Of selfless giving in God's sight.
Her name none can recall.

On Calvary's hill, where passions stirred,
A nameless one that day
Sought pardon from the dying Lord,
Who promptly gave the promised word
Which speaks to us today.

More Than These

When recognition and acclaim
Are given sparingly,
Think that your deeds and not your name
Give value to the good you claim.
A nameless angel be.

Desmond E. R. Ottley

(41) OBEDIENCE

When struck with dread disease,
He to the prophet came
Expecting quick release
Appropriate to his name.
But Naaman's pride his healing stayed,
Till he obeyed and faced the tide.

All night in useless toil
They fished and nothing caught.
Frustrations seemed to boil,
Their labour was for naught.
But then the Lord a plan unveiled,
And they obeyed, and praised His word.

Breaching the roof above,
Kind friends the lame man brought.
Unable even to move,
A healing cure he sought.
Him we adore great power displayed;
The lame obeyed and sealed his cure.

The wine supply went dry
At Cana's wedding meal.
With water resupply,
Said Jesus, with much zeal.
They spread the word which was relayed,
And they obeyed, and all were served.

More Than These

When life's woes press us down,
Or pride obstructs our path,
When disappointments drown
Our hopes, and nurtures wrath,
Then learn to pray and put your trust
In Christ the Just. His words obey.

When life's wine jars run dry,
Or health gives way to pain,
When dreams we value high
Prove joyless, without gain,
Then learn to pray and put your trust
In Christ the Just. His will obey.

(42) *Immediately or Wait?*

God's love is pure, redemptive, all-embracing.
God's power is irresistible and sure.
The Will Divine submits to no resisting,
The Power Supreme its purpose will ensure.
Results may flow at once, or lie in waiting
Until God's timepiece strikes the appointed hour.

The suppliant leper came, and he was healed.
The wayside blind men had their sight restored.
The mother-in-law of Peter, sick and fevered,
Was by His tender touch, instantly cured.
The widow's son with burial shroud all covered,
Was raised to life, awakened by God's word.

All these received their blessing without waiting.
But God's wise ways often demand delay.
The faithful Abraham, firm in believing,
Saw not the hoped fulfillment in his day.
But God, whose word is steadfast and unchanging,
Fulfilled the promise, just as God did say.

Consumed with jealousy, his vengeful brothers
Tried cruelly to rid themselves of him.
They bound and gagged him, selling him to others,
Making young Joseph's future dark and dim.
But in the end, despite the evil powers,
God rescued Joseph and his father's kin.

More Than These

In my own life, challenged by joy and sorrow,
I'll praise and trust my Lord each wondrous day.
Whether relief comes now or some tomorrow,
I'll trust God's love, and I my vows will pay.
Convinced a Godless life is vain and hollow,
I'll trust in God, till death. Let come what may!

Desmond E. R. Ottley

(43) *Fruitful Habits*

All along life's pathway, silently obscure,
Treacherous traps of habit dormant lie,
Gaining strangling footholds, dangerous to the core,
Waiting your good manner to defy.

Will you in your bosom hide a poisonous snake,
Knowing of the damage it can cause?
Why then nurse resentment? Why such wrong path take,
Knowing this defies life's proven laws?

Will you keep a vicious tiger in your home,
Knowing of its penchant to attack?
Why then in your heart let hateful thinking roam,
Knowing hate will give no good thing back?

Why still keep desires for revenge alive
When the wrong has long forgotten been?
Why keep harbouring grudges rather than forgive?
Spurn these attitudes! Live life that's clean!

So what if you are right and the other wrong,
Why make such a needless federal case?
Someday you'll be weak, the other will be strong,
And you'll have pride's egg upon your face.

All along life's pathway golden chances lie,
Calling you to take the higher road.
Practice fruitful habits; they will edify,
And will help to lighten many a load.

(44) Immediately

In this life of care and challenge as we strive our best to give,
We receive abundant signals questioning the way we live.
Some we ignore with abandon, some we boldly may disdain,
Others seek our prompt responses and produce immediate gain.

As they tended to the mending of their fishing nets that day,
They could hear the Master saying "Follow Me, walk in My way",
Not for them the weak excuses that so often stunt our growth.
They dropped all and quickly followed, sealing an unspoken oath.

Has the Master called you lately? Has the Spirit prompted you
To respond with quick obedience to the signal in plain view?
Have you turned from all the clutter that has clogged your life till now,
Following Him from dawn till darkness, with His hand upon your [plough?

As they sat beside the wayside, blind, discouraged by their plight,
They could hear the Master passing; they knew He could give them [sight.
So despite the stormy protests from the unrelenting crowd,
They cried out to Him for healing and they instantly were cured.

Are you blinded by life's stresses, or discouraged in your quest
To find peace and calm and healing mid the world's ingrained unrest?
Though the world by its unfriendly effort may distract your view,
You can call on Him in person and receive your healing too.

He was clearly told by angels how to name his promised son.
But he doubted the fulfilment, and from that day he was dumb.
When the moment came as foretold, he obeyed and wrote the name
That the angel being had given. Instantly he spoke again.

When life's puzzling situations leave you drenched in unbelief,
When the answers to your prayers provide no comfort or relief,
That is when, with new conviction, you must trustingly obey
Signals to your conscience given. Trust in Him who is the Way.

More Than These

(45) Cut The Rope

Losing his foothold, he began to fall,
Down from the icy ledge at treacherous height.
The rope held fast, but none would hear his call,
As dangerously he tumbled in the night.

With sudden jerk, still hanging from the rope,
He fell no more; but knew with certainty,
That without urgent help he had no hope
Of rescue from this sore calamity.

His dangling feet cried out for solid ground.
His eyes were darkened by the frigid night.
His body yearned for even a distant sound,
But nothing surfaced to resolve his plight.

Then wishfully he said a silent prayer,
And instantly he heard a calming voice
Which said: "Just cut the rope, you need not fear."
But full of fear, he made a faithless choice.

He did not cut the rope. But at first light
His rescuers in their search his body found
Frozen and lifeless, 'twas a painful sight,
Hanging just five feet above solid ground.

Do we, like him, pray earnestly at length,
But when the answer comes, in disbelief
We spurn its message, trusting in our strength,
That we could somehow find our own relief?

Desmond E. R. Ottley

Our prayers are heard, no matter where they're said.
The answer always comes, you can be sure.
With ears and eyes and insight, Spirit led,
We will receive what's needed to endure.

Let us with trusting hearts, give thanks and praise
When victories come and joy-cups overflow.
But when disaster strikes, still let us raise
Our grateful voice, and faithful actions show.

(46) Drifting

Down at the beach, how soothing is the feeling,
When you lay floating on some buoyant planks,
Enjoying sounds from nearby waves a-breaking,
And looking upwards, ponder, and give thanks.

Then suddenly you see that you're in danger;
The tide has slowly pulled you far from land.
You must return, you can delay no longer,
Else ne'er again would your live feet touch sand.

So in life's journey, when we start enjoying
All the rewards that our successes bring,
If we forget the source of our receiving,
We will start drifting even as we sing.

Not overnight, nor by a single action,
Do we stray from the straight and narrow way.
But by neglect that's frequent with inaction,
We slowly drift till we are far away.

A faith-filled life requires daily nurture,
As does a garden threatened by strong weeds,
Which, if not culled, would choke the floriculture,
And all around spread their unwanted seeds.

Our spiritual armour can't be left unguarded
If we desire that it remains secure.
We daily must ensure that it's safeguarded
By virtuous deeds, by kindly thoughts and pure.

Desmond E. R. Ottley

Daily do battle 'gainst unseen invaders
That surreptitiously attack the soul.
Living as if we are indeed joy-makers,
Anchored, not drifting, faithfulness our goal.

(47) God's Temple

In many lands around the world
Some ornate temples have been built,
Displaying wealth and beauteous art,
Sometimes depicting human guilt.
But each one, whether great or small,
Is sanctioned by the Spirit's call.

Our bodies sacred temples are,
According to God's Holy Word.
Our faith demands we keep them clean,
A wholesome dwelling for our Lord.
An undefiled and sacred place,
A residence of saving grace.

We need to guard the body's gate
Wherein may enter impure thought.
We need to post, ere it's too late,
A watchful guard that has been taught
To turn away each dangerous foe
That would inflict disabling woe.

The games we play, the food we eat,
The carefree pleasures we enjoy,
The way we care our hands and feet,
The daily habits we employ,
These must enhance our body's health,
Else we will gain just worthless wealth.

Desmond E. R. Ottley

Our words, our thoughts, our minds and more
Must be in keeping with this goal;
To be as sacred and as pure
As scripture says should be our soul.
So that our bodies will remain
God's temple, ready for His reign.

(48) Not All Chains

When ships in port are threatened by strong tides,
They are secured by chains tied to their sides.
The carnival lion and the harmless ape
Are bound by chains, preventing their escape
    To freely roam.

The dangerous convicts are securely bound
By chains wrapping their hands and feet around.
All these, despite their efforts and desires,
Are held at bay, just as inflated tires
    Are kept in check.

But not all chains, restrictive though they be,
Are made from metal. One can surely see
That hardened habits, groundless fears and dread,
Can paralyze intent and leave as dead
    Our wisest plans.

The Great Designer meant us to be free
To soar above, to live abundantly.
But often we allow those self-made chains
To bind our thoughts and stifle many gains
    That we have won.

We craft our plans and know how to proceed.
Yet we procrastinate and kill the deed;
Or we prejudge how critics will oppose
The steps we take, and prematurely close
    The open door.

Desmond E. R. Ottley

We thwart the emergence of our moral strength
By fostering envious thoughts, which will at length
Give rise to kindred foes like greed and hate,
Destructive chains which leave us in a state
    Of hapless woe.

O that we all may banish from our minds
The selfish thinking that so often binds
Our kindly will. May we, with purpose strong,
Commit ourselves to vanquish all the wrong
    From self-made chains.

(49) DECISIONS

Each day we make decisions
That govern all we do.
We try our best to make them
Conform to what is true.
Yet there is none among us
Who has not missed the mark,
And made a wrong decision
That birthed a dangerous spark.

Sometimes we make decisions
Without deliberate thought.
At times we do much thinking,
Using truths we've been taught.
Sometimes the moment calls us
To sudden, quick response,
Giving no time to ponder
The best way to advance.

How can we plan our living
So that each day and night
Is built on wise decisions
That guide our steps aright?
How can we gain assurance
That all our words and deeds,
When planted in life's garden,
Become fruit trees, not weeds?

Desmond E. R. Ottley

We need to truly practise
The wise truths we have learned;
The truths that Jesus taught us,
Which often we have spurned.
Take time to read and ponder
More prayerfully each day
How best to apply these gemstones
To guide us on life's way.

What does our God require,
That we in faith may give
Ourselves to true obedience,
And to His glory live?
God asks that we live justly;
That we with mercy treat
Our fellow-human beings,
And walk with humble feet.

(50) BEFORE DAYBREAK

When will I find the time to sing and pray,
Time to be spent alone in secret thought?
Time to lay bare my soul to God each day,
Time to receive the guidance I have sought?

Each day's demands fill all the allotted hours;
Dealing with family needs, duties at work,
Keeping routines, scant time to smell the flowers,
My days get filled with tasks I fear to shirk.

But at day's end, I sense an empty space.
Today I spent no time in prayer to God.
I lived without a single thought of grace,
No thought to give back even a thankful nod.

This fault I must correct ere it's too late.
I must find time each day to spend in prayer,
Seeking forgiveness, learning how to wait
For daily strength and guidance, battling fear.

If I can't daily find the time to pray,
I can with diligence follow Christ's lead.
Whene'er He sensed ahead a busy day,
He rose before daybreak, on prayer to feed.

This plan may tax my physical will each morn,
And furnish weak excuses to withdraw
From gaining needed blessing, ere the dawn
Gives way to care and toil—life in the raw.

Desmond E. R. Ottley

With reasoned care I can retire each night
Early enough to gain a full night's sleep,
And wake refreshed before the dawning light,
With time enough my prayerful watch to keep.

It all depends on where I've set the bar;
Whether I'll monitor the global woes,
Or give attention to each spiritual scar
Which by my own neglect I self-impose.

No one on earth but me can re-direct
My errant course that leads away from God.
But my best effort cannot resurrect
The strength and will I need to stay the road.

Therefore with firm resolve and all my power,
I will each day take time to sing and pray.
Whether at dawn or dusk or midday hour,
Through joy or tears I'll pray. Let come what may!

(51) I THANK YOU SAVIOUR

For all Your gifts, remembered or forgotten,
For all Your love shown through Your Son begotten,
For all your kind forgiveness for each failure,
    I thank You Saviour.

For Your forgiveness when my words were spoken
Without much thought for hearts that may be broken,
For daily pardoning my unkind behaviour,
    I thank You Saviour.

For overlooking times I have not trusted,
Banking instead on my own strength, though rusted;
For always helping in my daily labour,
    I thank You Saviour.

For opening doors when I've faced disappointments;
Providing friends in grief, like precious ointments,
Sharing my joys and woes, lending your kind favour,
    I thank You Saviour.

All that I ever needed You've provided,
Even when my thoughts and Yours at times collided.
For being my strength and hope, even in disaster,
    I thank You Master.

Both now and always, I will trust You deeply;
No more distractions from my worship daily.
For blessing me in everything I do,
    Dear Lord I thank You.

Desmond E. R. Ottley

(52) WHO ARE WE TO COMPLAIN?

We sometimes spend much time in vain complaining,
Whether it's summer's heat or winter's cold.
We fret about the dampness when it's raining,
Yet fret when drought-stressed buds fail to unfold.

Christ said we must face life as little children,
Eager to learn, not fearing bruising falls.
They get around by creeping, then by walking,
Ere long they're running chasing birds and balls.

They have scant knowledge of the world around them,
Stretching each day the boundaries of their mind.
Meanwhile they deeply trust their loving parent
To be protective, amiable and kind.

God is all-wise, all-powerful and all-knowing.
God's love transcends all human wish or thought.
God made the natural systems we depend on;
All that we need God's gracious hands have wrought.

Compared to what God knows, we do know nothing.
Alongside God's great power, we helpless are.
God heeds our doubts and questions, and is patient.
So to complain is going a bit too far.

God knows the universe that has been forméd
By the Divine Command and Wise Design.
The choices that I make are mine to fashion.
But in the end God's will is done, not mine.

More Than These

Trust in the Lord. You run no risk so doing.
God's word is true and faithful to the last.
Give first place in your life to your divine Guest.
No more complaining! Let your faith hold fast.

Desmond E. R. Ottley

(53) TWO MORE DAYS

Sometimes when we are troubled sore,
With anxious thoughts and sighs, and more,
    When bane and bliss collide,
We turn in prayer to touch the One
Who promised we'll not be alone,
    If we in Him confide.

With unfeigned fervour we reveal
Our inmost fears, and we appeal
    For aid from the Divine.
Oft we expect that right away
The help will come without delay,
    To stem the tide, in time.

At times no answers we receive.
Our worsening state makes us believe
    No timely aid will come.
But answers come each time we pray;
For though they may not come today,
    God's will must sure be done.

Recall the message that was sent
To Jesus with such grave intent;
    "Your friend is very sick".
There was no doubt that when He heard
The unhappy news, He would be stirred;
    His coming would be quick.

More Than These

It wasn't. Two days He waited there,
As if He really didn't care
    About his dying friend.
But at the God-appointed hour,
Wrapped with compassion, love and power,
    He went! A blesséd end.

God chooses when and how to mend
Our fractured lives, and in the end
    Provides the cure that's best.
God's timing brooks no human guide.
With wisest love, God will provide
    The best for each request.

Desmond E. R. Ottley

(54) AS HE SAID

"Fear not! I know" these words were plainly spoken.
"He is not here, He's risen as He said".
Such joyful news revived their spirits, broken
By expectations they would find him dead.

Fear not! Christ knows the doubts you often ponder.
"I'm the Good Shepherd, and I know my sheep".
Just trust these Words; there's now no need to wonder
How you'll survive. Give faith in Christ a leap

Fear not! Christ knows the heartaches that depress you.
"Let not your heart be troubled" He has said.
Just trust this promise which was meant to soothe you,
And give clear vision by which you'll be led.

Fear not! Christ knows the wounds your spirit suffers.
"Be of good cheer. I've overcome the world".
You will receive the gifts which act as buffers
'Twixt you and hurtful shafts against you hurled.

Fear not! Christ knows you need divine protection.
"I will be with you even to the end".
If you would trust this promise of compassion,
Be sure all others will on you descend.

More Than These

(55) LEAVING WATERPOTS BEHIND

When that day she met the stranger
At the well she long had known,
She was challenged without danger
By his language deftly sown.
To that well she often journeyed
To draw water or unwind.
But his words so touched her soul, she
Left her waterpot behind.

How could he, a total stranger,
Know her life so thoroughly?
How could he, with such conviction
Speak in tones so lovingly?
This must be the Christ long promised,
To bring sight to all who're blind.
If he is, then I will gladly
Leave my waterpot behind.

So it is when we meet Jesus
At the well on life's lone path.
We are humbled by his knowledge
Of our faults, our fears, our wrath.
By his probing he assures us
That his yolk is light and kind.
Moved by his sweet voice, we gladly
Leave our waterpots behind.

Desmond E. R. Ottley

Waterpots we carry daily
To the wells of want and need,
Filling them with things we cannot
Do without, and on them feed.
But when challenged by the Saviour
To accept the grace declined,
With contrition, may we gladly
Leave our waterpots behind.

May I have the sense that favours
Lasting good o'er fleeting mirth.
May I spend my time on ventures
That will boost my neighbour's worth.
Governed by the kingdom's graces,
May I have my faith refined;
So that, at the last, I'll gladly
Leave life's waterpots behind.

(56) The Anchor

What is that crude and shapeless piece of metal
Hanging outside that fine ship's stately bow?
It mars its sleek and beautiful appearance.
It should be hidden far from view below.

It is the anchor, ready to be lowered,
Should storm-whipped waves threaten the ship to sink.
It digs through sand and grips the rock securely,
Holding the craft atop the watery rink.

When comes the storm and boisterous winds are howling,
The ship is tossed like seaweed on a pond.
But now that crude and shapeless piece of metal
Is lowered, and works its magic like a wand.

Despite the wicked waves and tortuous tempest,
The anchor safely holds its floating load.
The once disdained, detested piece of metal
Is now the only hope of those aboard.

So often this is how we treat Life's Anchor,
Whose power and love and wisdom we ignore,
Until the storms of life begin their onslaught
'Gainst our frail craft we felt was so secure.

If we are wise, even then we'll lower faith's anchor,
Though we have never yet affirmed its worth.
For Christ forgives even those who spurn His favours;
He modeled this when He lived here on earth.

Desmond E. R. Ottley

It's only when we feel the storm's full fury,
That we realize how deeply we depend
On whatsoever anchor we've established
To keep us safe when treacherous storms descend.

Christ is the only anchor that can keep us
Safe and secure through every storm we face.
He may not calm the deadly winds and billows,
But He will safely keep us by His grace.

You can, my friend, depend on Christ as Anchor;
But you must first allow Him full control.
Let every crevice of your life be governed
By His divine desire to make you whole.

Abandon all the wily props that keep you
Suspended on perfidious beds of ease.
Make Christ the Anchor for your troubled vessel.
He longs your fears and worries to erase.

(57) PRAYER

O God, our Comforter, our Friend,
The source of all we have or need,
Your loving wisdom hath no end,
You give the food on which we feed.
Fountain of life, teach us each day
How best to live, how best to pray.

You promised us ere You left earth
That You'll be always at our side.
Your word You've kept. But wealth and dearth
Often pervert our will to abide
Close to Your side. We often pray
As if 'tis You, not we, who stray.

Your word declares Love is Your name.
Your love for us transcends our thought.
Nothing but good, could we proclaim,
Comes to us, wanderers You have sought.
Yet repetitiously we pray
As if Your love has lost its sway.

All knowing Lord, God only wise,
You urge us to approach Your throne,
To ask and knock and seek with eyes
That trust Your deep wise love alone.
Yet knowing this, we turn to you
And pray as if this is untrue.

Desmond E. R. Ottley

Lord teach us how to pray aright,
That in our quiet prayer-time hour,
We may receive that inward sight
Which truly trusts Your love and power.
Imbue our minds, each night and day,
With faith-filled thoughts whene'er we pray,

(58) DRAW US BACK

With great excitement they had heard
His invitation to desert
Their fishing nets; and at His word,
Without even sending an alert
To those at home, they instantly
Went with Him, following faithfully.

For several years o'er hill and dale,
On dusty roads, with weary feet,
In stormy seas, through mountain trail,
Beset by hunger, cold and heat,
They journeyed. All the while He showed
How best to walk the Godly road.

Their lives were changed. His words and deeds
Taught them deep spiritual truths with power.
These truths sank in their minds like seeds
Sown in the earth, to grow and flower.
But heinous deeds on Calvary's hill
Ruined hope like a poisonous pill.

Their loss was great. Their pain was sore.
An aching void now filled each heart.
A sense of hopeless musing tore
Their heartstrings, piercing like a dart.
Forgetful of the truths they learned,
Back to their fishing nets they turned.

Perhaps, like them, there was a day
When you responded to God's call
To follow Christ. Without delay
You yielded, and in faith stood tall.
The Master's Way became your own,
His garment's hem on you was sown.

Obedience to the Word became
Your daily goal, your nightly prayer.
To walk in faith was your chief aim,
To trust His wise and loving care.
But now, alas, lukewarm and weak,
Your faith no more His mercies seek.

Perhaps it was some grave event
That touched your life and caused you pain.
Perhaps, o'er time, your days were spent
In an illusive search for gain.
These you allowed to infiltrate
Your peace, through an unguarded gate.

Fear not! Hold on! He loves you still.
He knows the pained regret you bear.
Though carelessly far from His will
You've strayed, He bids you now draw near.
He comes, as then, to draw you back,
And yearns to resupply your lack.

Let God work wonders in your life.
Open the door to faith again.
Refuse to let doubt use its knife
To distance you from God's good reign.
As sure as daybreak follows night,
God's love will always be your light.

(59) COME UNTO ME

Do you enjoy your life each day and hour,
Or are you often like a wilted flower
That lacks the moisture needed to survive?
Hear One who calls, your spirit to revive,
    "Come Unto Me."

If you are thirsting for a new approach
To deal with those who silently encroach
Upon the areas that affect your peace,
Trust One who calls, your courage to increase.
    "Come Unto Me."

He promises that you will surely find
Rest for your soul, and peace, the lasting kind.
Bright skies may darken still, and storm clouds lower.
But if you trust, you'll find these words give power.
    "Come Unto Me."

Some say "I am the captain of my soul".
Others believe they are in full control.
Yet none can claim full mastery over all
That vexes life. So heed the urgent call:
    "Come Unto Me."

Come Unto Me, if tired and worn out.
I'll show you how to turn your life about.
Stay with Me, learn the gentle force of grace.
With Me you'll learn to walk with surer pace.
    "Come Unto Me."

Desmond E. R. Ottley

I'll teach you things you never thought could be.
You'll see beyond the vistas you now see.
I'll take your hand and show you paths to tread
That will enhance you life and lift your head.
    "Come Unto Me."

THE END

"God will give you all you need

from day to day

if you live for Him

and make

the Kingdom of God

your primary concern."

[Matt. 6:33 New Living Translation]

INDEX of Meters, Titles and Scriptural References

<u>Poem</u>   Meter / Title / Scriptural Reference
The numbers in [—] represent the meter of a suitable hymn tune
The number in {-} represents the Title number of the poem

Poem	Meter / Title / Scriptural Reference
After the wedding	[8.7.8.7] {33} Eph 4:26
And Peter	[8.7.8.7.7.7.7.7] {29} Mark 16:7
As He said	[11.10.11.10] {54} Matt 28: 5,6, 20; John 10:14; 14:1; 16:33
As I	[8.7.8.7.D] {19} John 15:10 & 12
Before Daybreak	[10.10.10.10] {50} Mark 1:35
Breaking down barriers	[8.7.8.7.D] {39} Matt 5:38-39
By the wayside	[7.6.7.6.D] {16} Matt.20:30
Claims of Jesus	[11.10.11.10] {12} John 10:9; 14:6; 6:35; 15:5
Come unto Me	[10.10.10.10.4] {59} Matt 11:28-30
Consider the stars	[8.8.8.8.8.8] {4} Ps 19:1
Cut the rope	[10.10.10.10] {45}
Decisions	[7.6.7.6.D] {49} Micah 6:8
Draw us back	[8.8.8.8.8.8] {58} Matt 4:19-20; John 21: 3, 15
Drifting	[11.10.11.10] {46} Eph. 6:11
Even in a dream	[10.10.10.10.4] {10} Matt. 1:20; 2:12-13
Follow Me	[12.11.12.11] {30} John 21: 19-21
Fruitful Habits	[11.9.11.9] {43}
God's love, wisdom ...	[6.6.11.6.6.11.D] {36}
God's temple	[8.8.8.8.8.8] {47} I Cor. 3:16-17
His garment's hem	[8.8.8.8.8.8] {17} Mark 5:25-34
Immediately	[15.15.15.15] {44} Matt 4:22; 20:30-34; Luke 1:13, 20, 63-64

Immediately or wait?	[10.10.10.10.10.10] {42} 2 Peter 3:8-9; Mark 1:40-42; Matt 9:27-30; 8:14-15; Luke 7:12-15; Gen 17:1-8; 37:18-28; 39:2; 45:8
Invitations from Jesus	[11.11.11.5] {13} Matt.11:28-30; John 21:12; Mark 6:31;10:21
It changes everything	[8.6.8.6.D or D.C.M.] {7} Matt.1:18-25; Luke 1:34–38
I thank You Saviour	[11.11.11.5] {51}
I was there	[11.10.11.10] {25} Matthew 26:3; John 19:8
Leaving waterpots behind	[8.7.8.7.D] {55} John 4: 28-29
Life's earthquakes	[10.4.10.4.10.10] {27} Acts 16:24-26 Matt.27:51
Nameless angels	[8.6.8.8.6] {40} 1 Kings 17:12-15; John 6:9; Mark 12:42-44; Luke 23:39-43
No room	[12.11.12.11] {8} Luke 2:7
Not all chains	[10.10.10.10.4] {48}
Obedience	[6.6.6.6.8.8] {41} 2 Kings 5: 1-14; Luke 5:5; Mark 2:3-12; John 2:1-10
On the road	[10.10.10.4] {26} Luke 24:13-35
Overcoming	[8.5.8.5.8.4.3] {38}
Prayer	[8.8.8.8.8.8] {57} Luke 11:1; 18:1; Matt 28: 20; 1 Thes 5:17
Prayer before Brunch	[8.7.8.7.8.7] {34}
Prayer for our nation	[8.7.8.7.8.7] {37}
Questions of Jesus	[8.7.8.7.D] {11} Luke 8:45; 17:17; John 6:67; 21:15
Roadblocks	[10.4.10.4.10.10] {2} Prov. 6:6; 30:25
Salt	[8.8.8.8] {5} Matt. 5:13
Stay with us	[11.11.11.6] {28} Luke 24:29
The amazing Christ	[8.7.8.7.D] {20} Matt. 12:13; Mark 2:11; John 2:1-10;
The anchor	[11.10.11.10] {56} Heb. 6:19
The beauty of God's world	[11.11.11.11] {1}
The Child from Bethlehem	[8.6.8.6 or C.M.] {6} Luke 1:79; 2:1-20
The day between	[8.7.8.7.3.3.7] {23} Matt.27:29-31; 28:18
The key to your heart	[11.10.11.10] {9}

The other Joseph	[8.7.8.7.D] {24} Gen.37:3; Matt.2:13; Mark 15:42-46
The pitcher of water	[8.7.8.7] {18} Mark 14:13-16
To whom shall we turn?	[9.8.9.8] {15} John 6:68-69
Trust in God	[10.10.10.10.10.10] {35} John 16:33; Philipians 4:19; Isa 43:2; Prov 29:25; 1 Kings 17:16; Matt 15:36; Dan 6:22; John 10:15
Two more days	[8.8.6.D] {53} John 11:6
Watch with Me	[8.8.8.D] {22} Matt. 26:38-40
Water	[11.11.11.11] {3} John 3:5; 4:13-14; 7:37-38
What a friend	[7.6.7.6.D] {21} Luke 12:7 John 10:9 Mark 15:34
What manner of man	[8.6.8.8.6] {14} Mark 4:37-41
Who are we to complain	[11.10.11.10] {52}
You promised Lord	[8.6.8.6.D] {32} Isa 65:24; Luke 1:79; Matt.7:7

Notes

Notes

Notes